I0468765

To Jean,

Thanks for all your support, knowledge, and insight on this project. Without your help, this coloring book would not have come to fruition.

Thank you

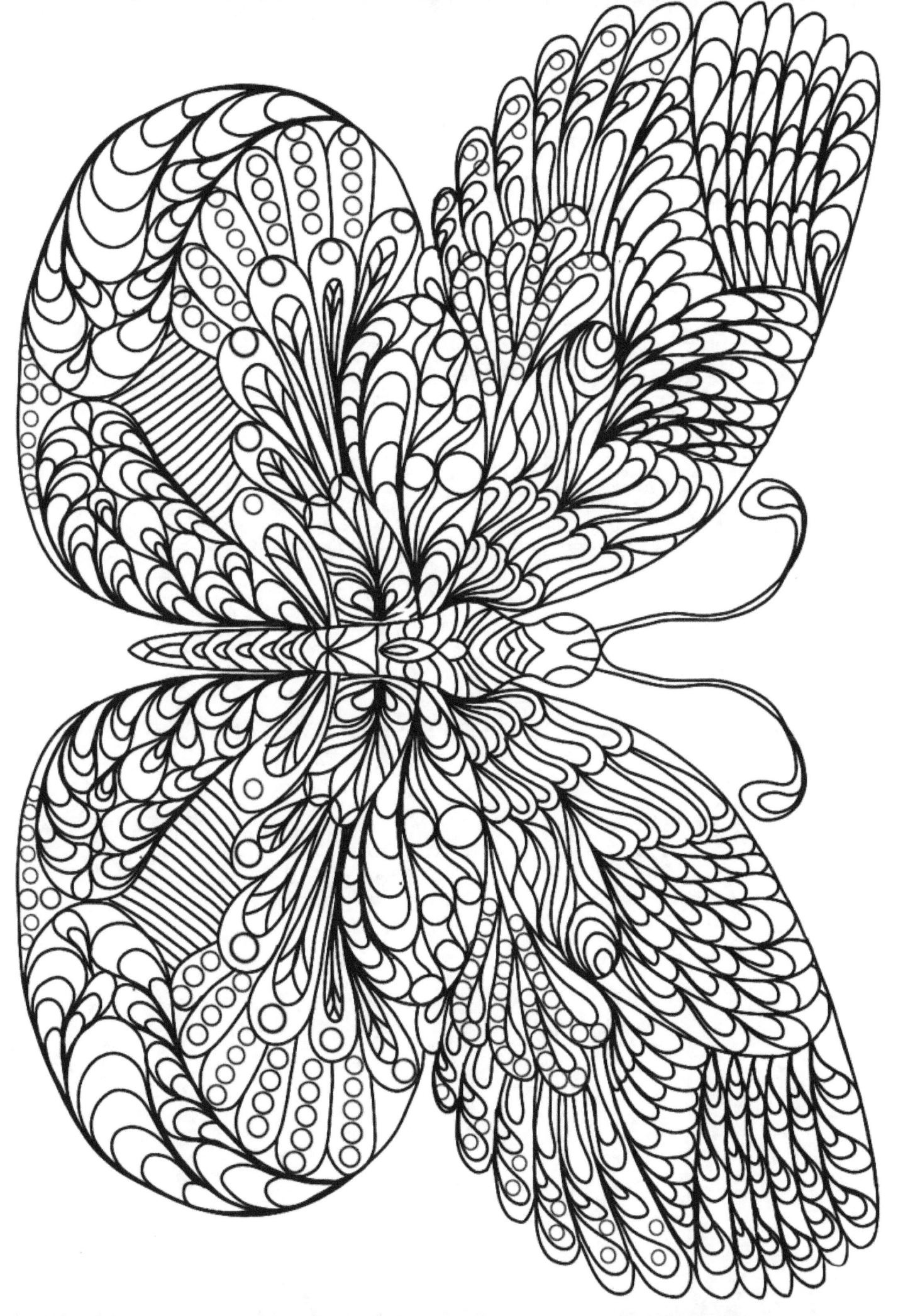

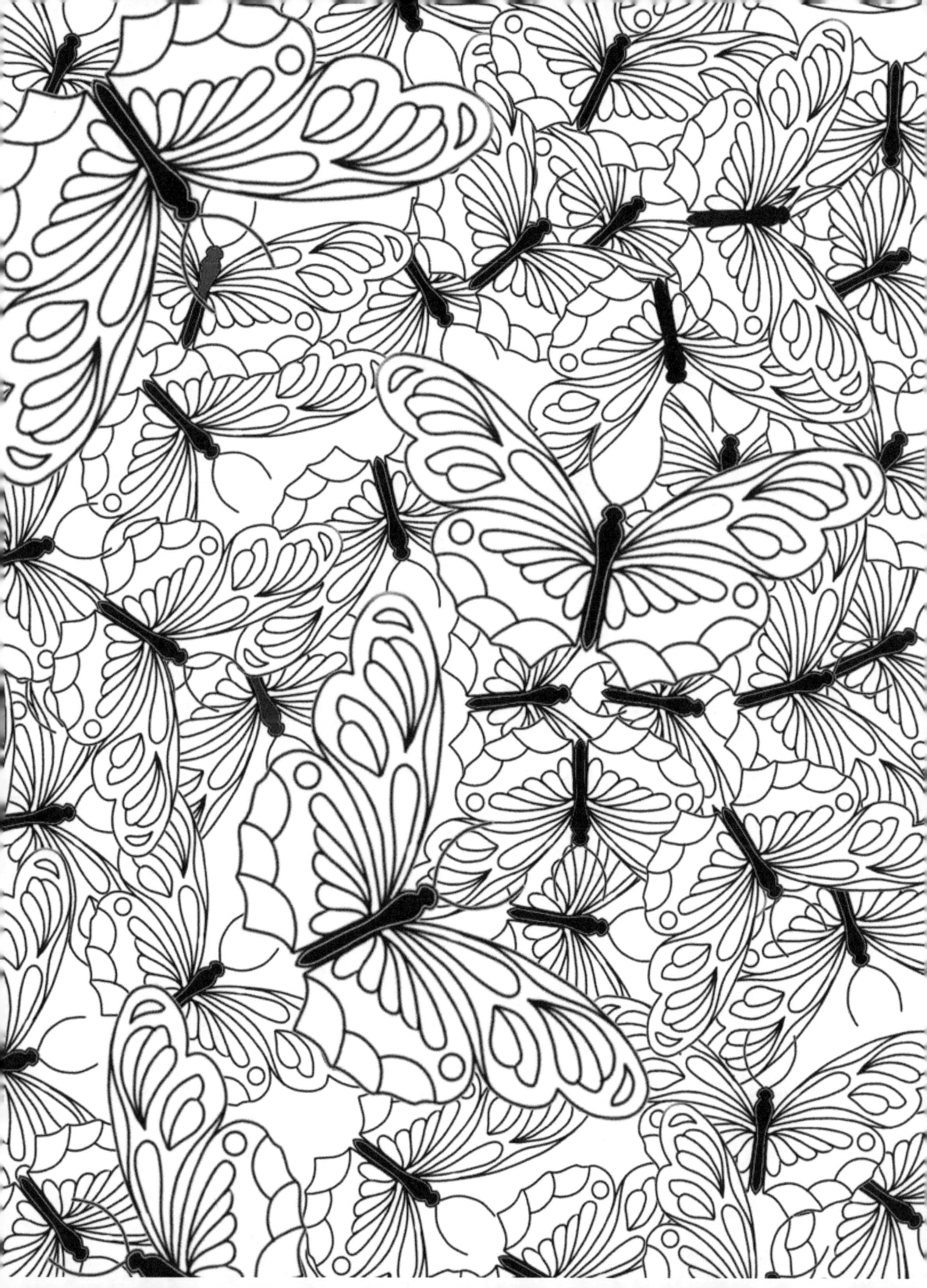

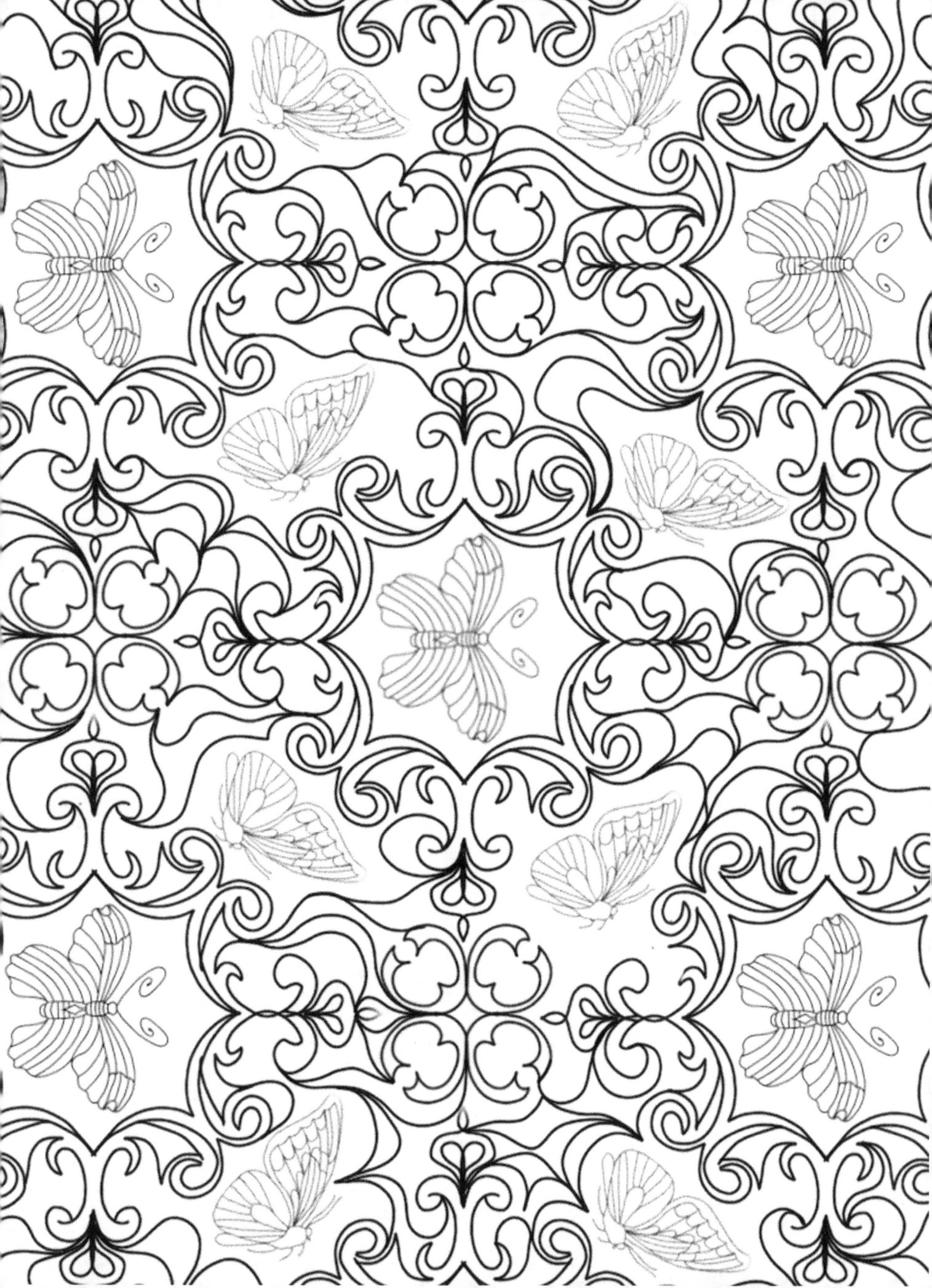

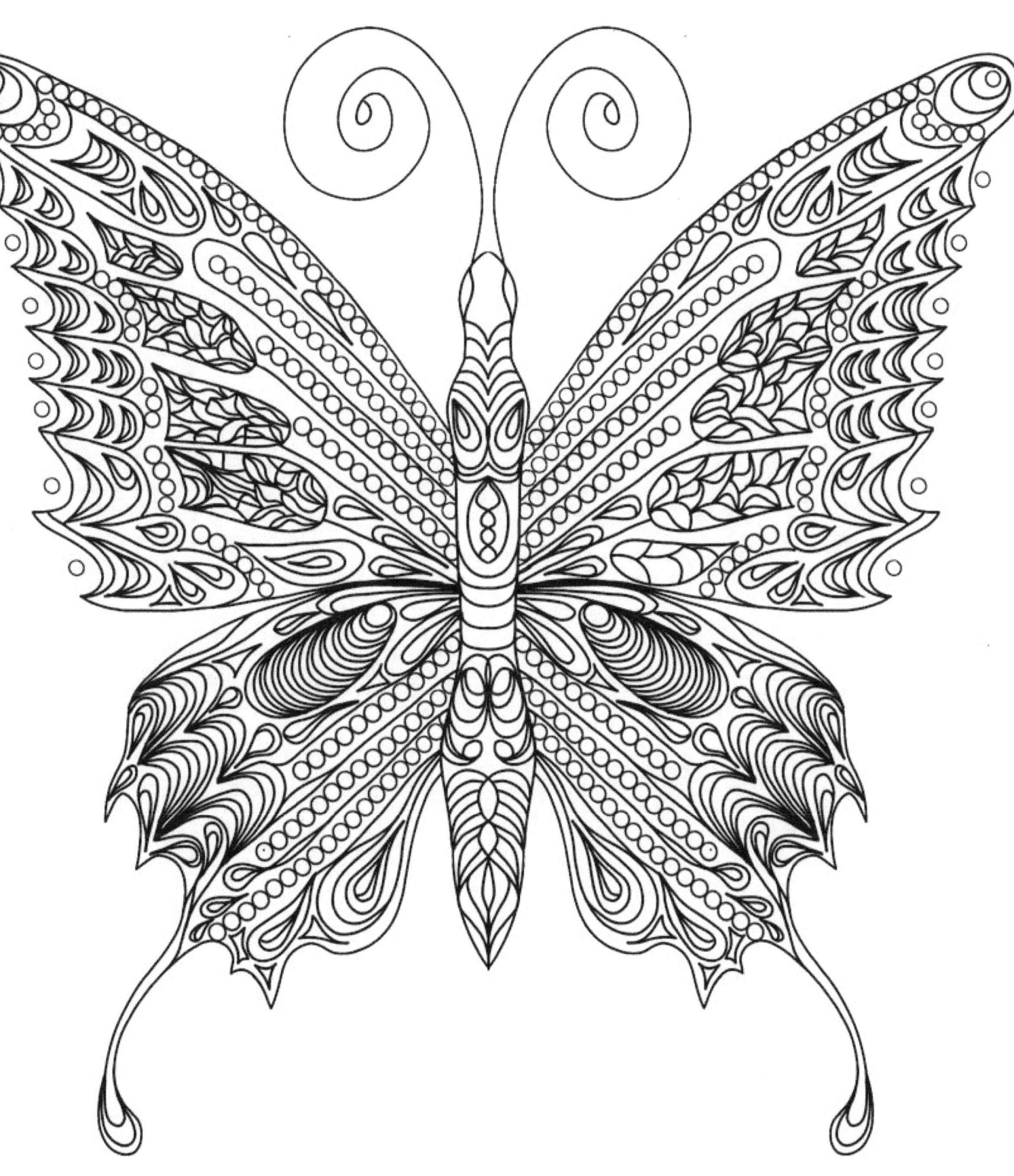

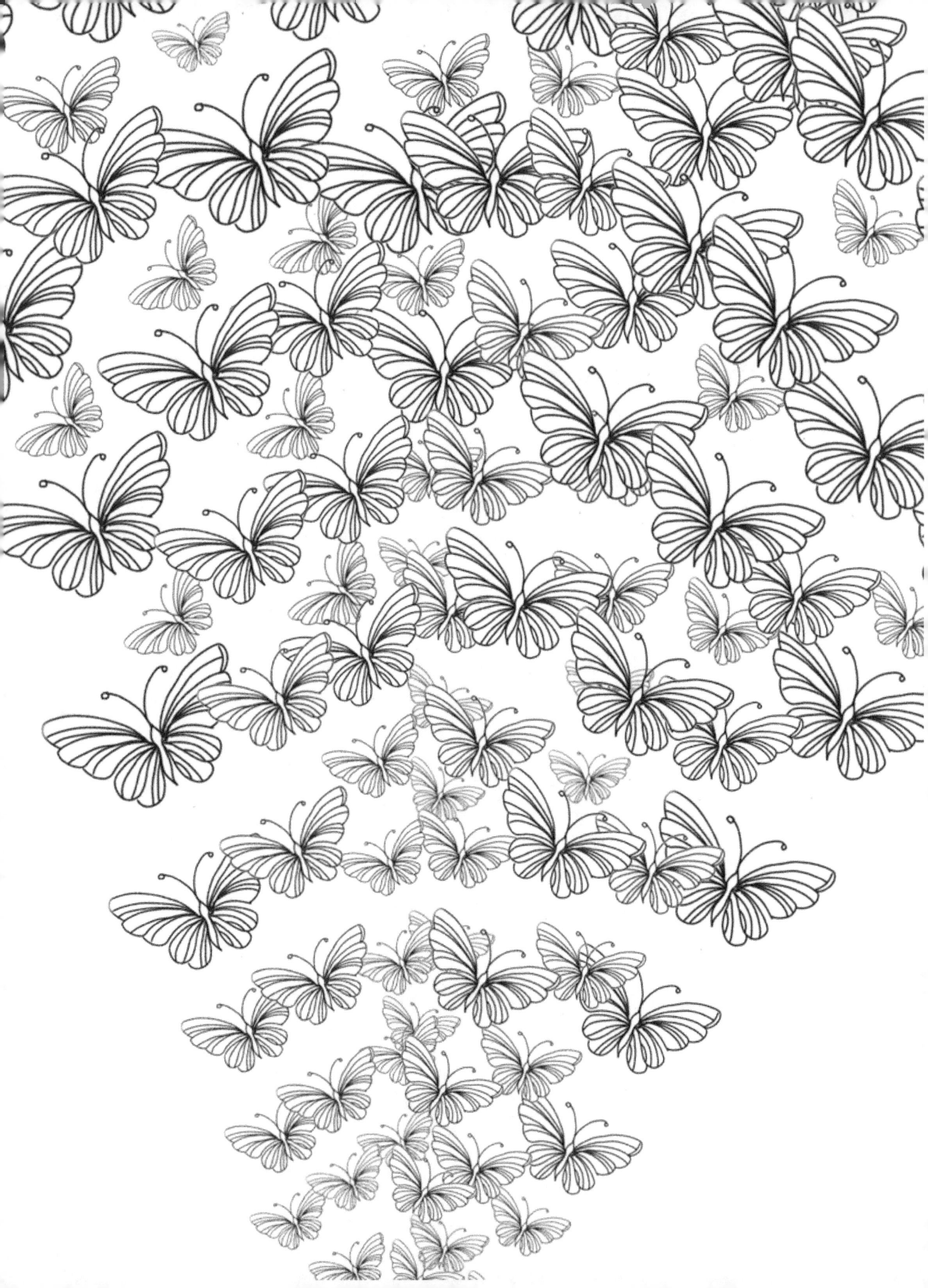

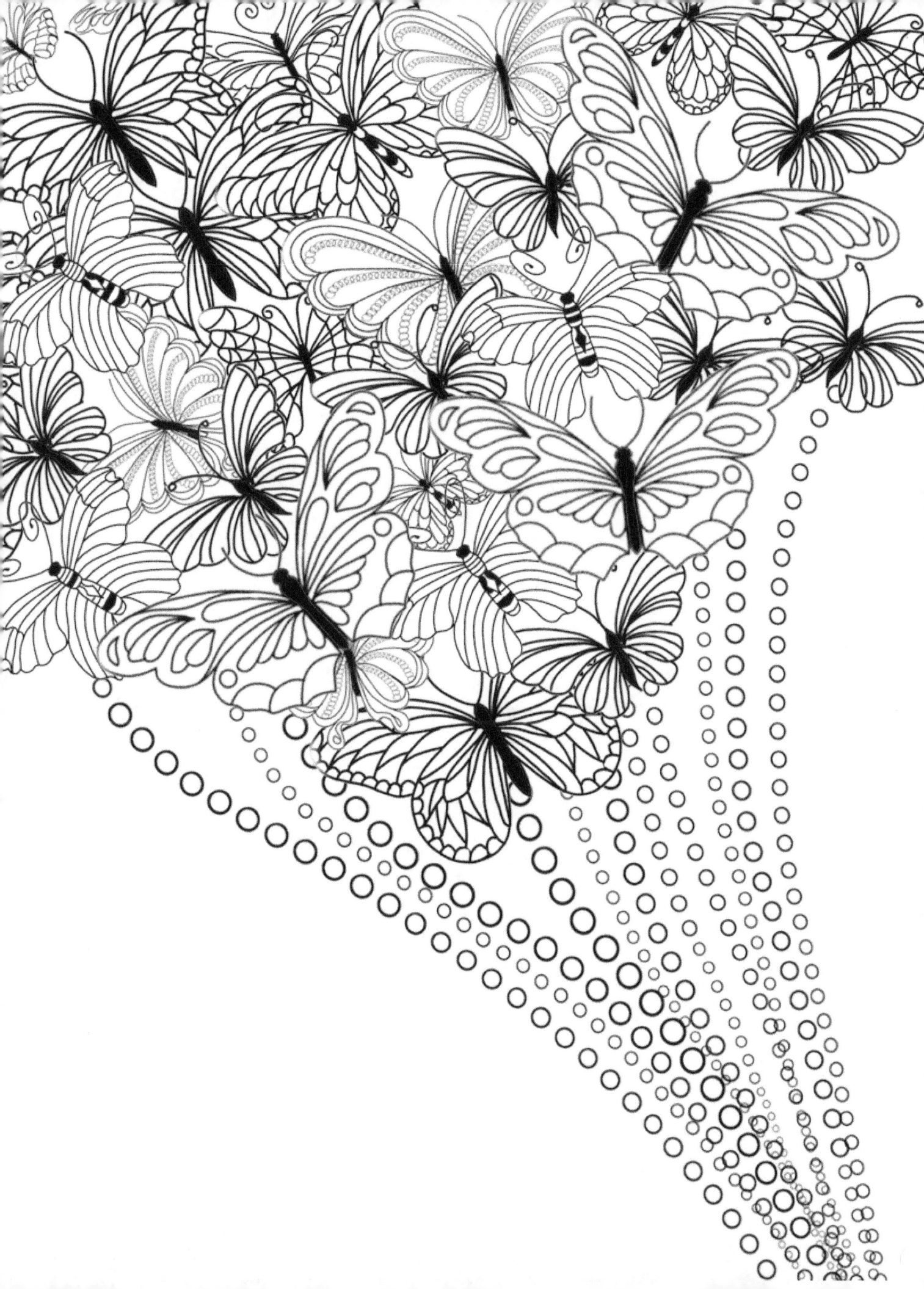

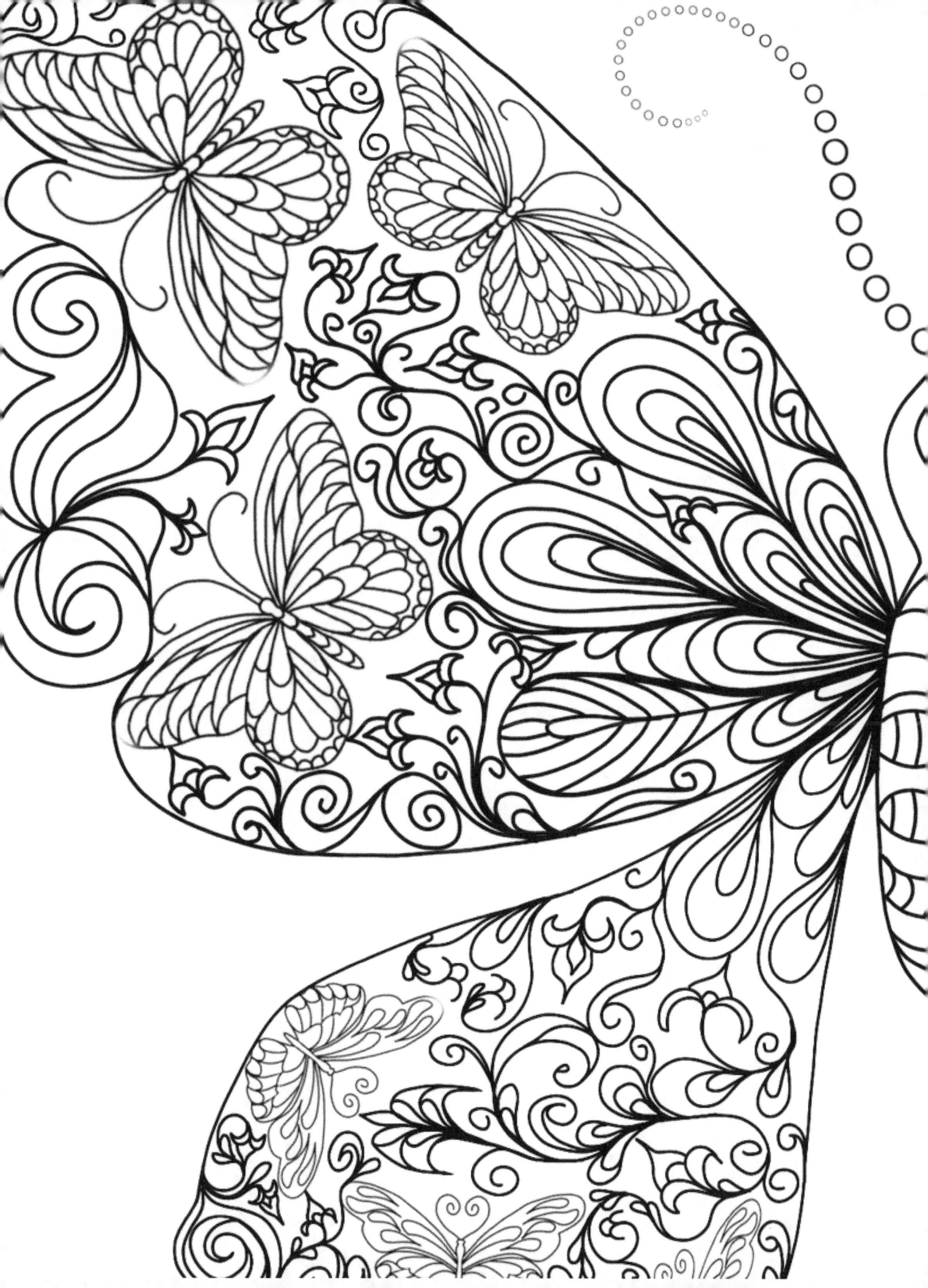

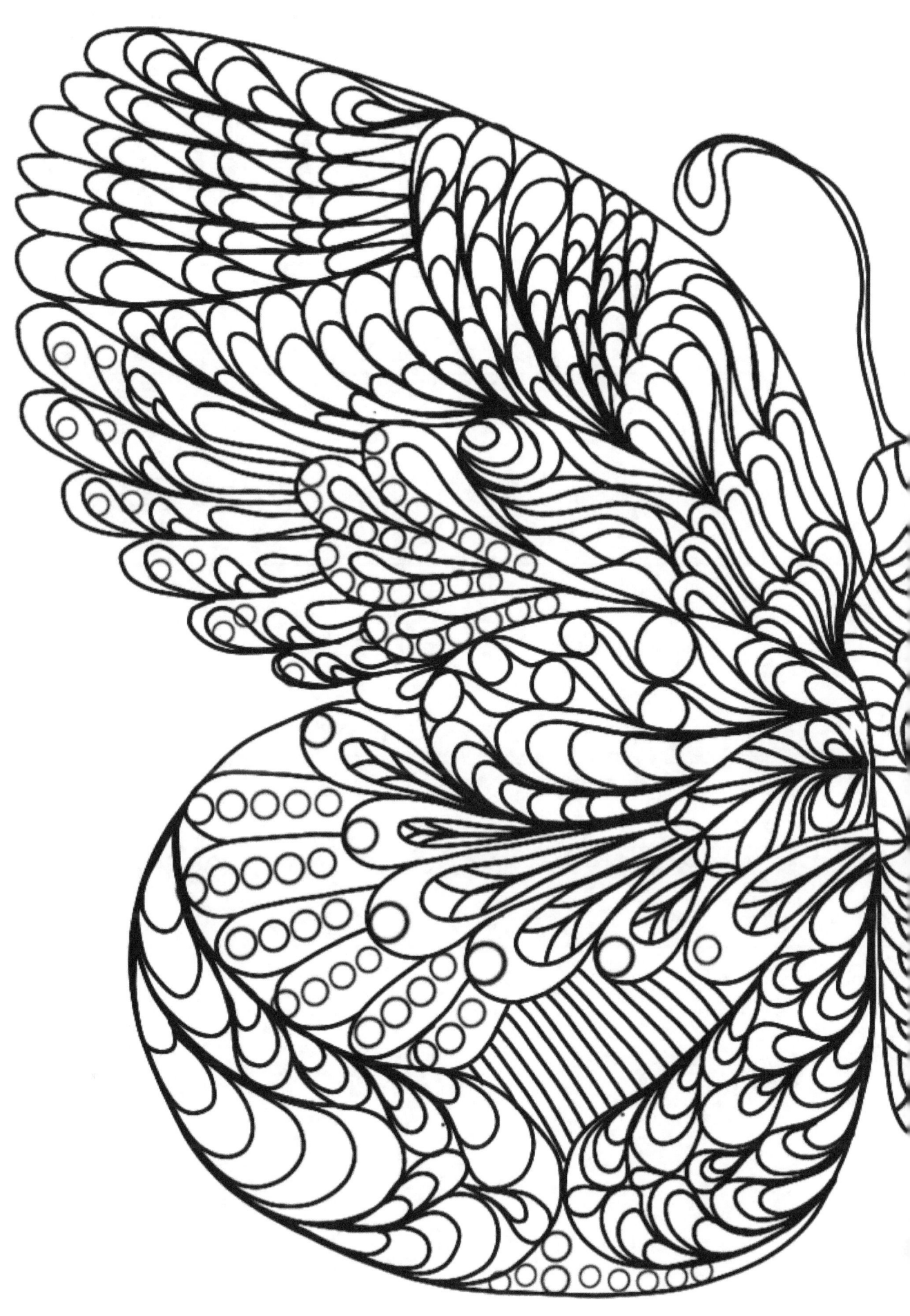

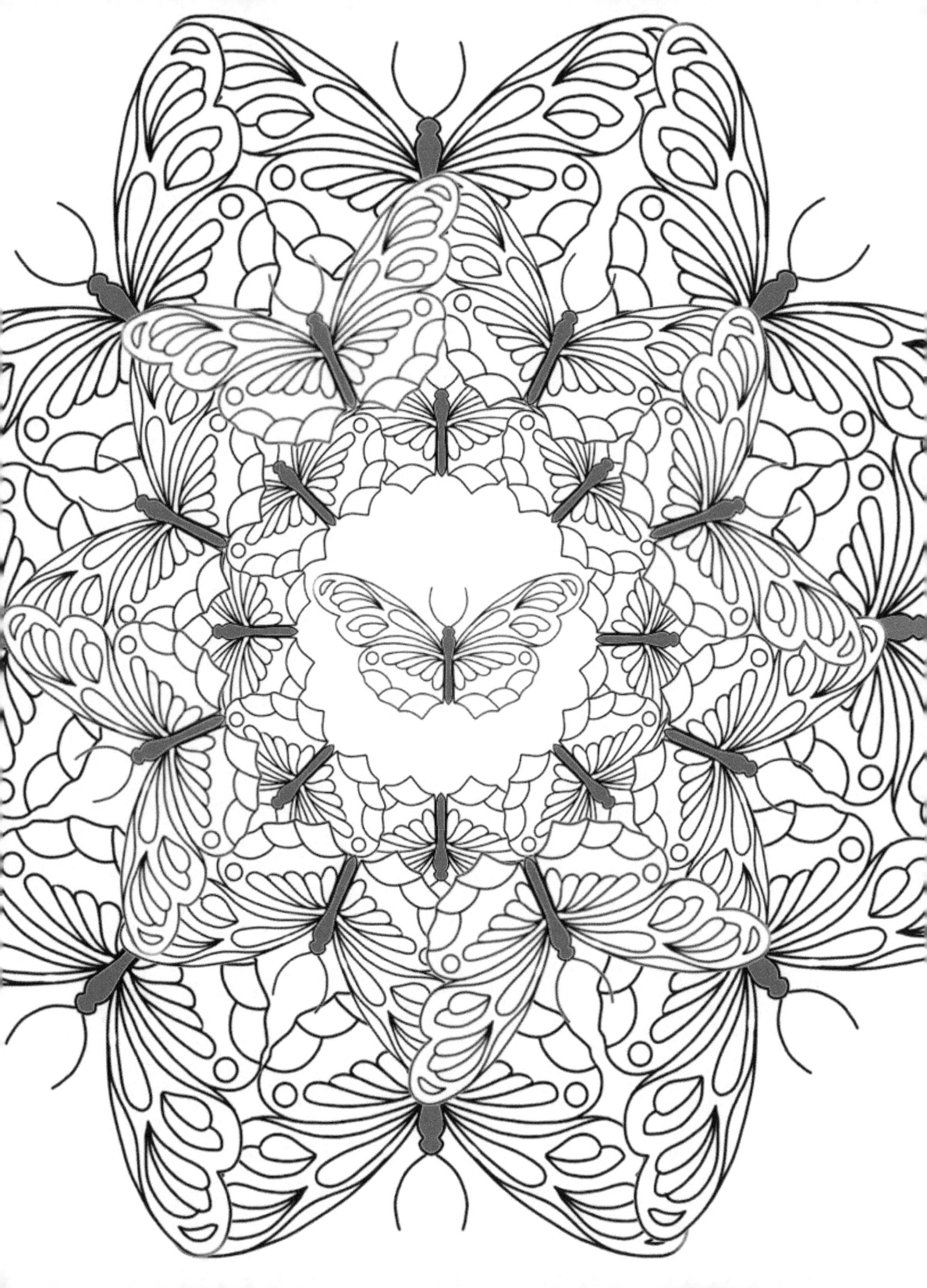

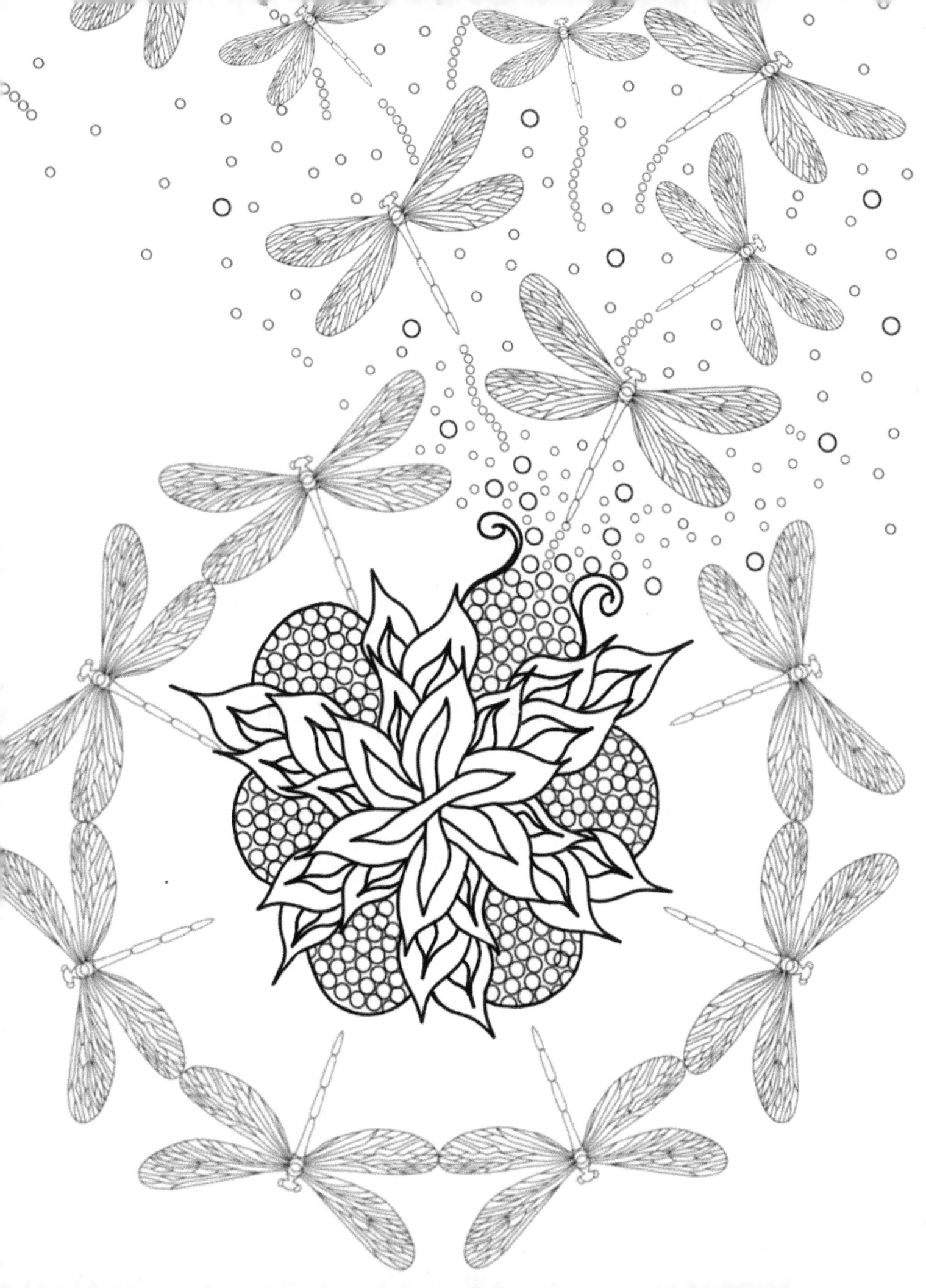

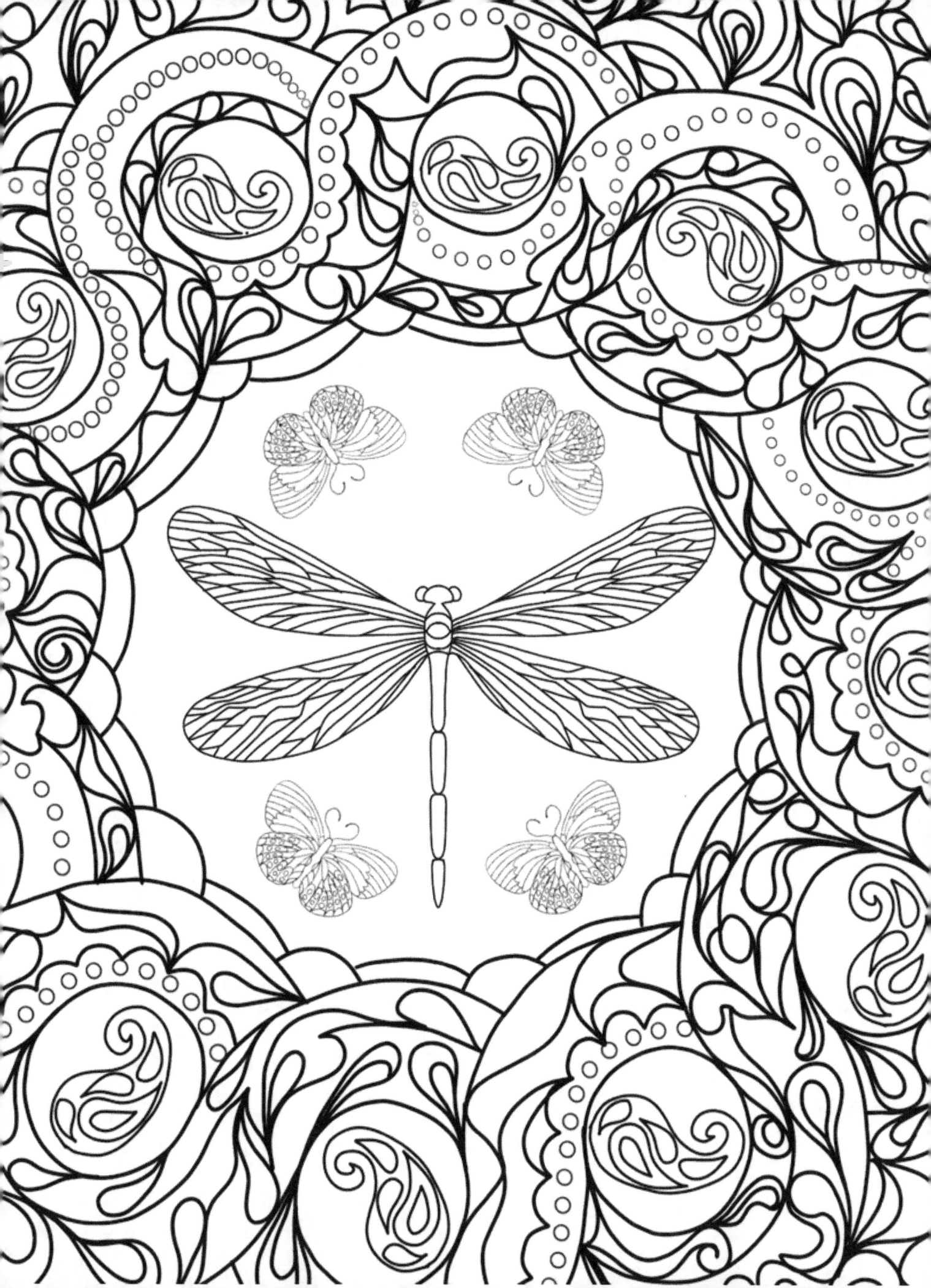

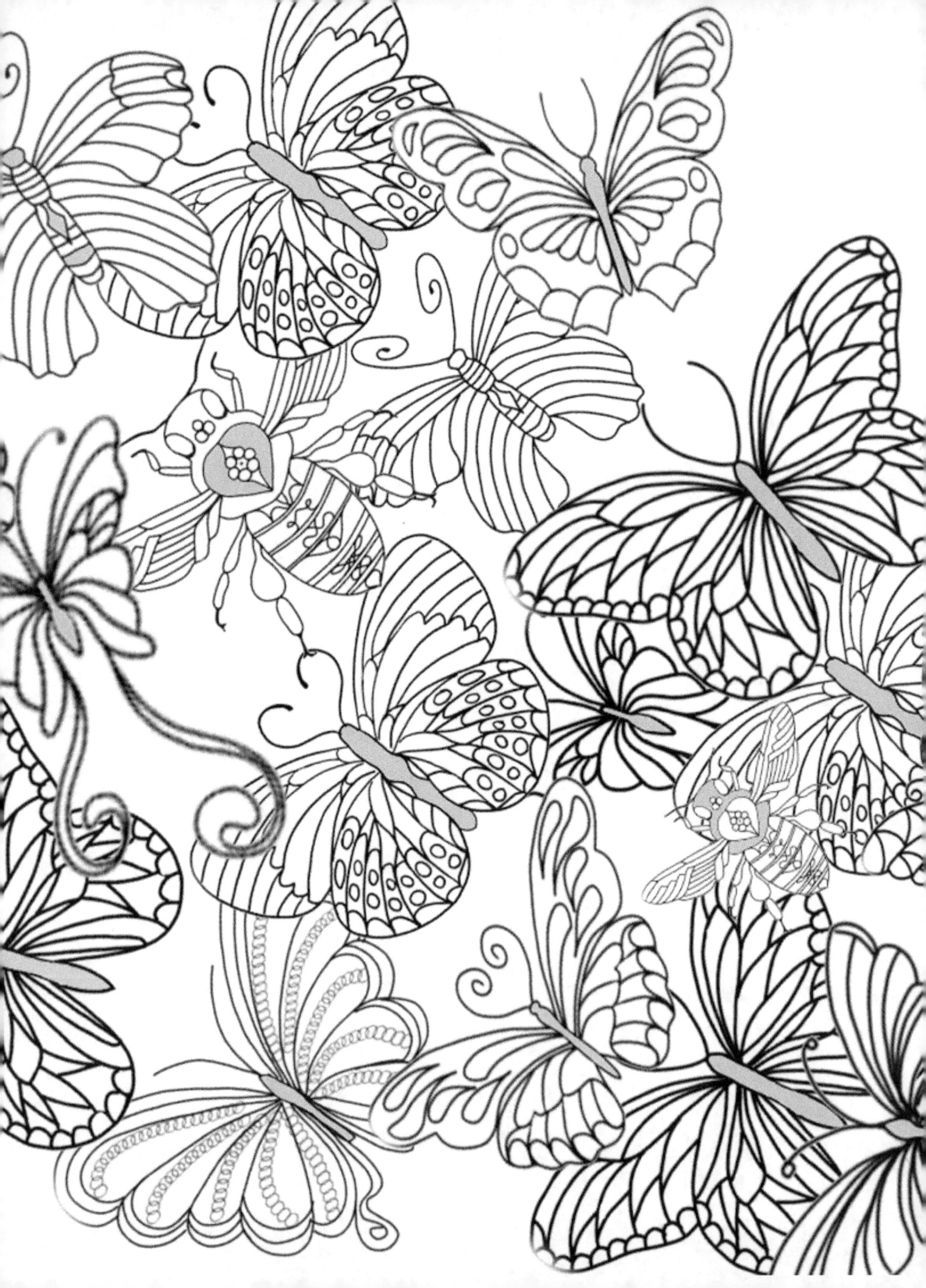

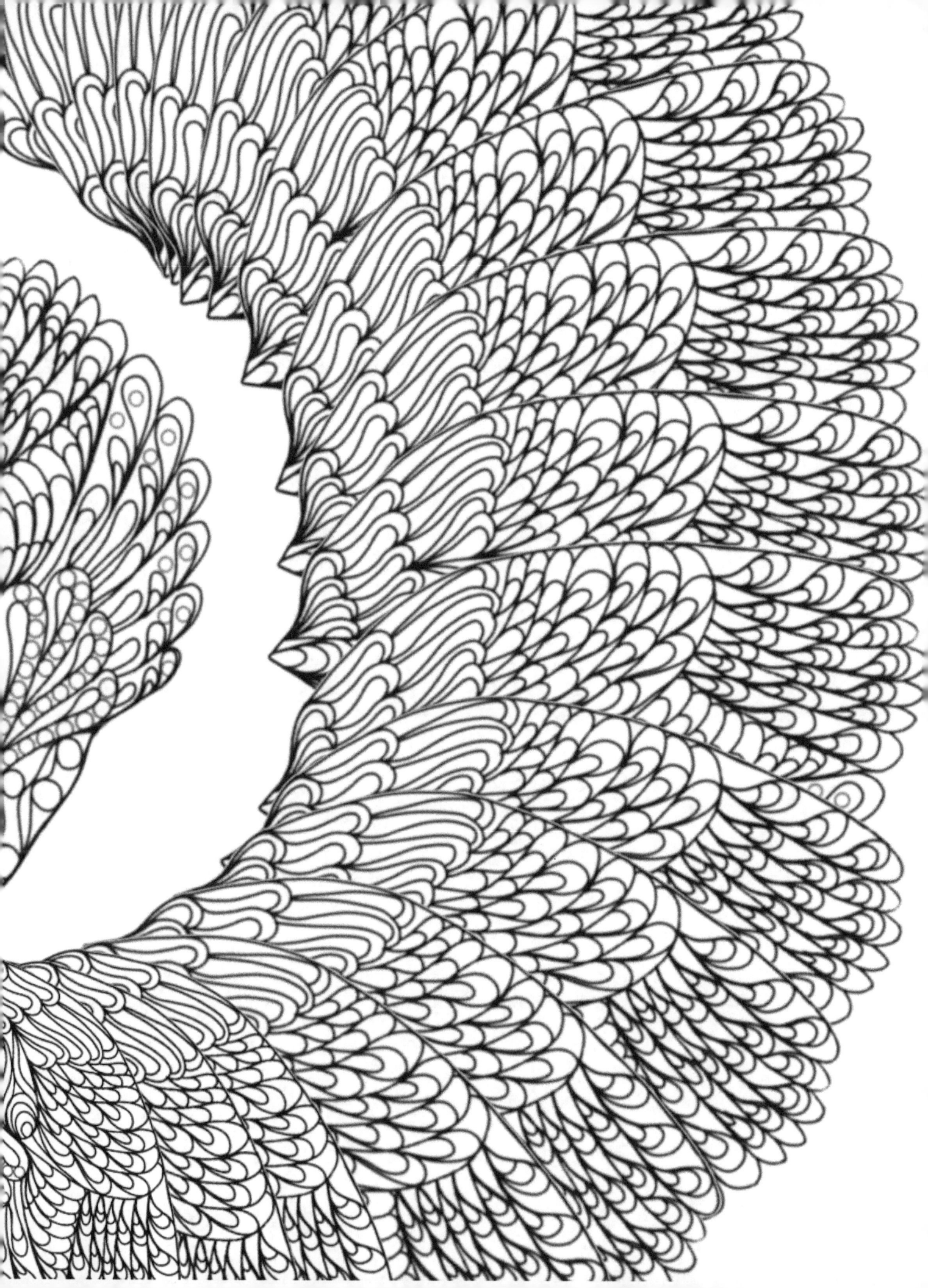

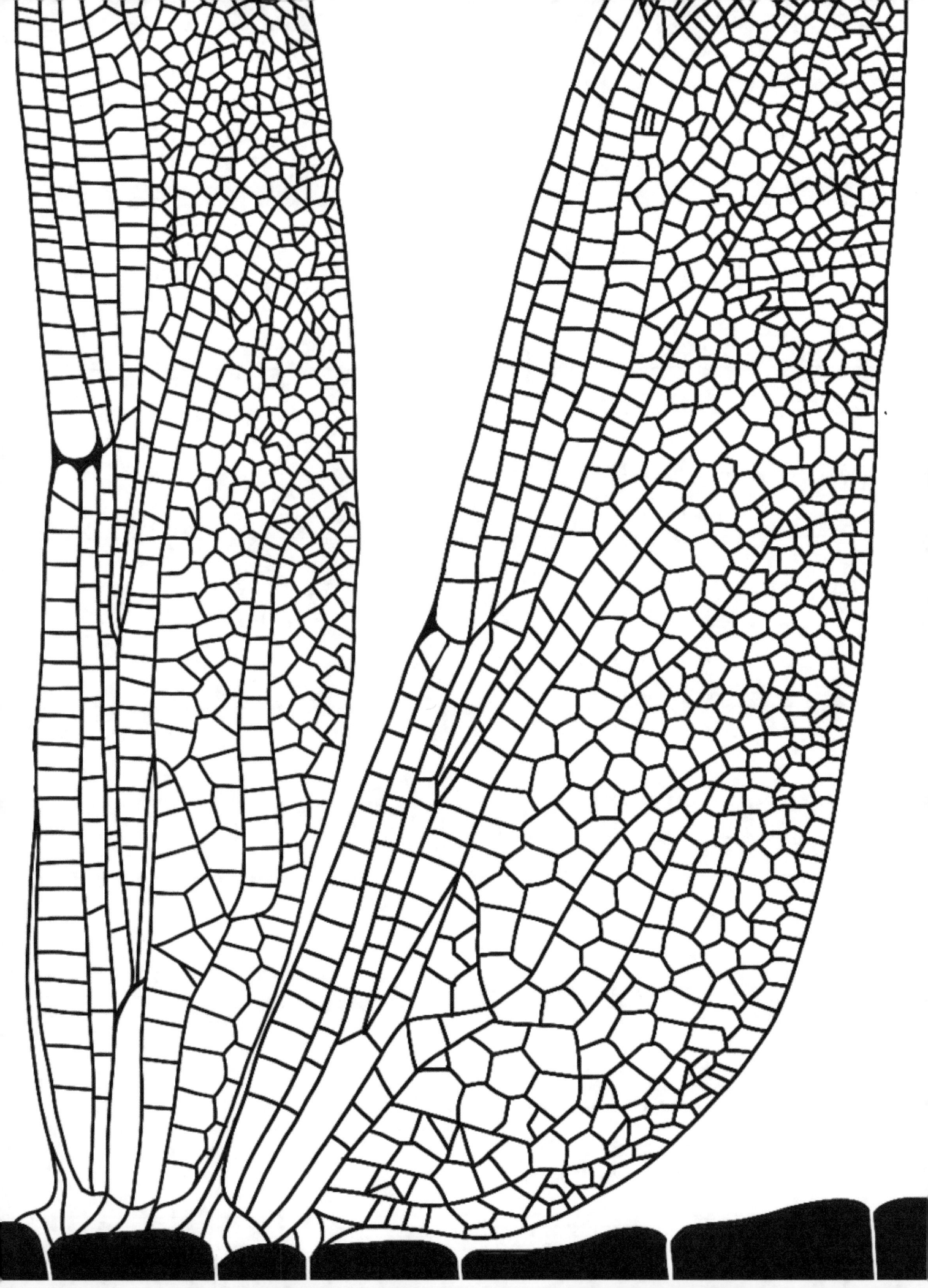

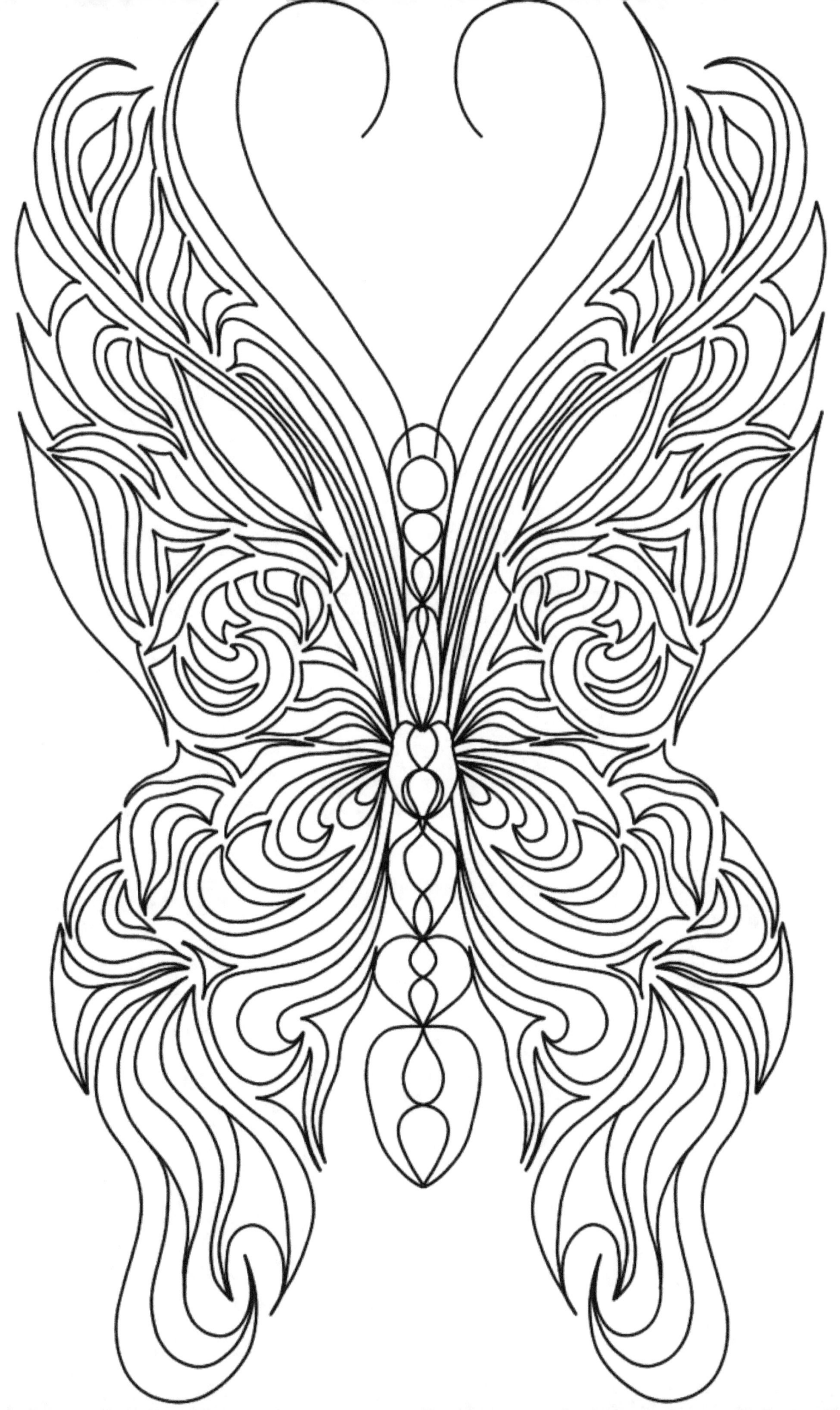

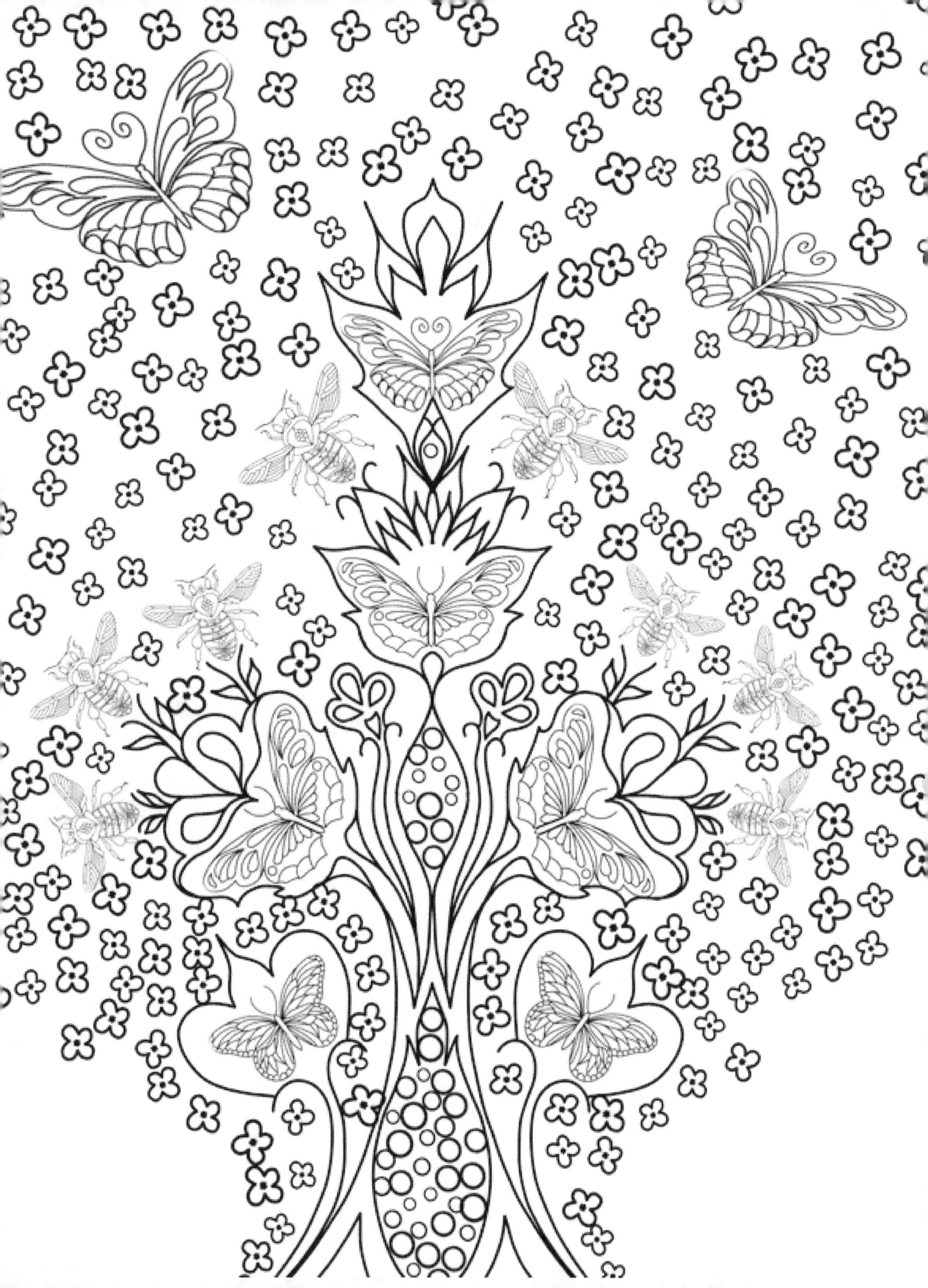

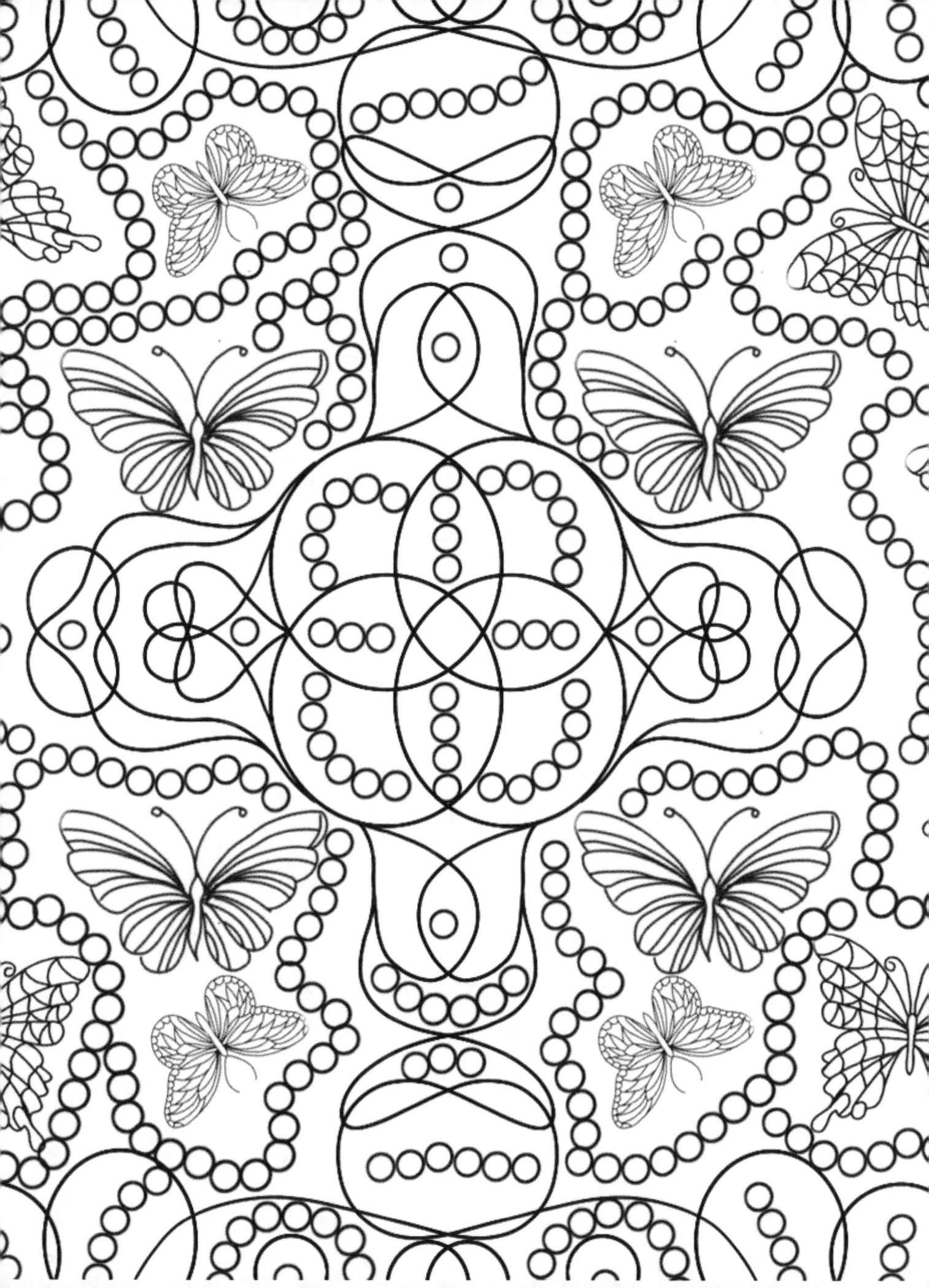

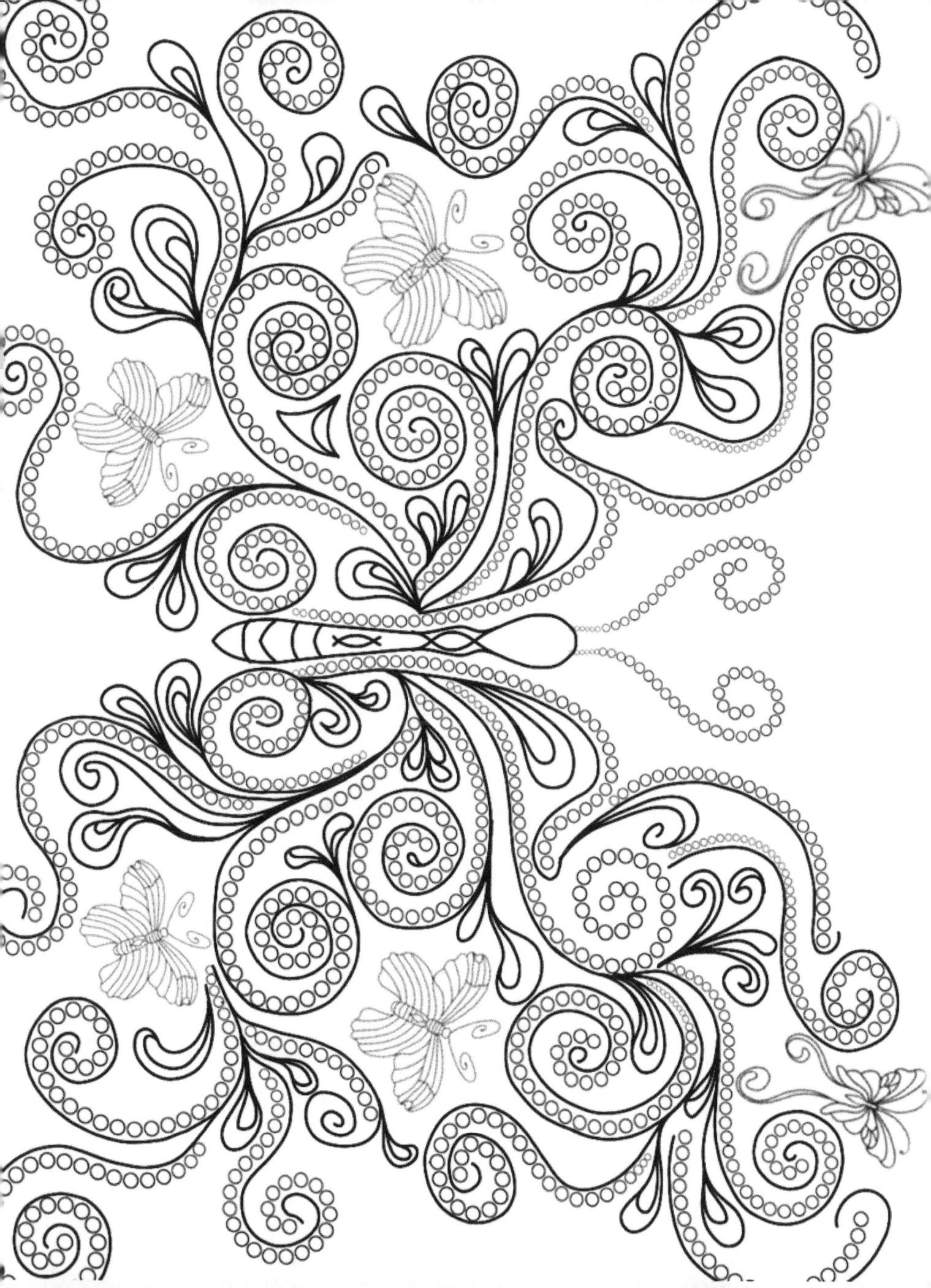

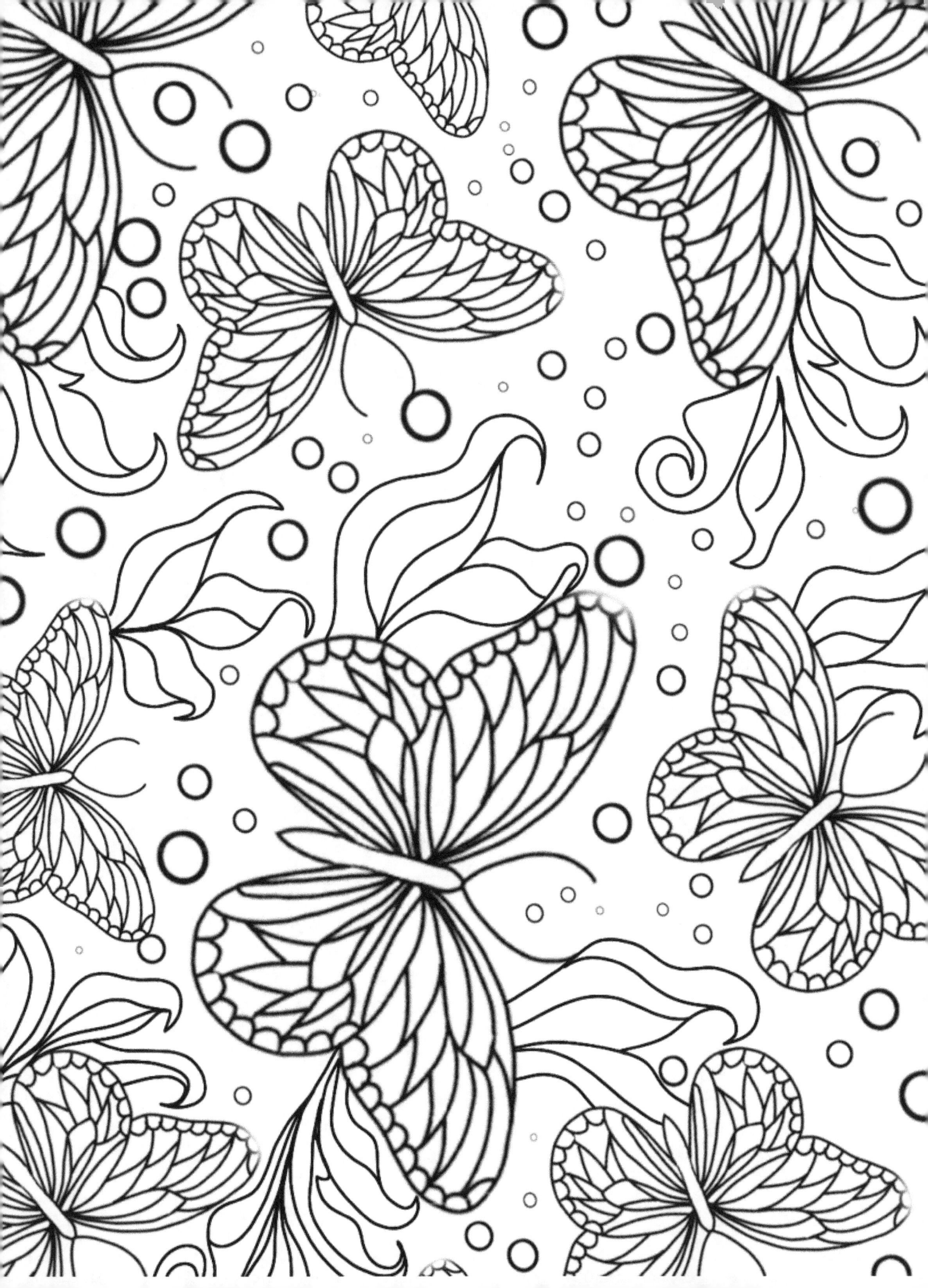

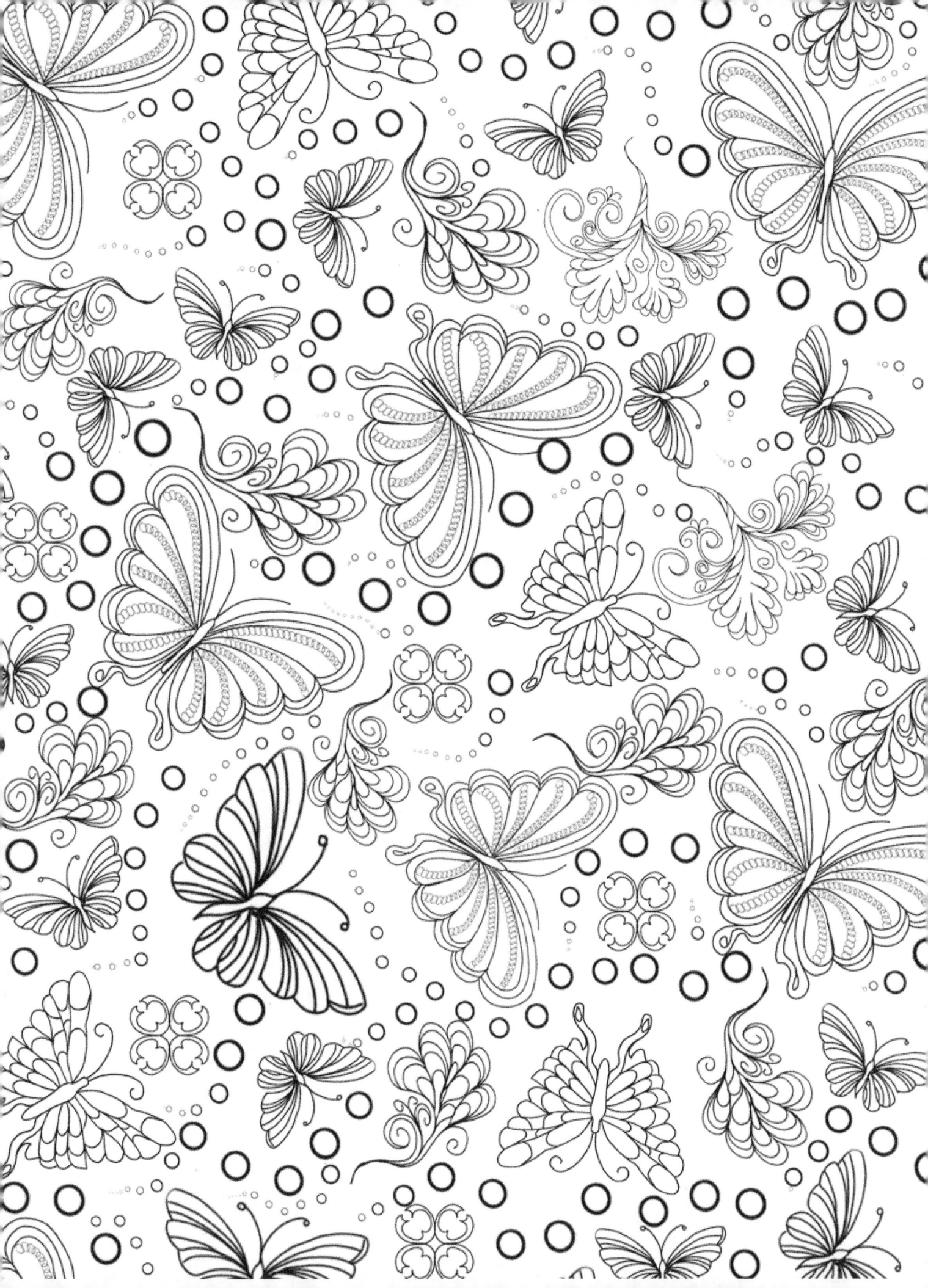

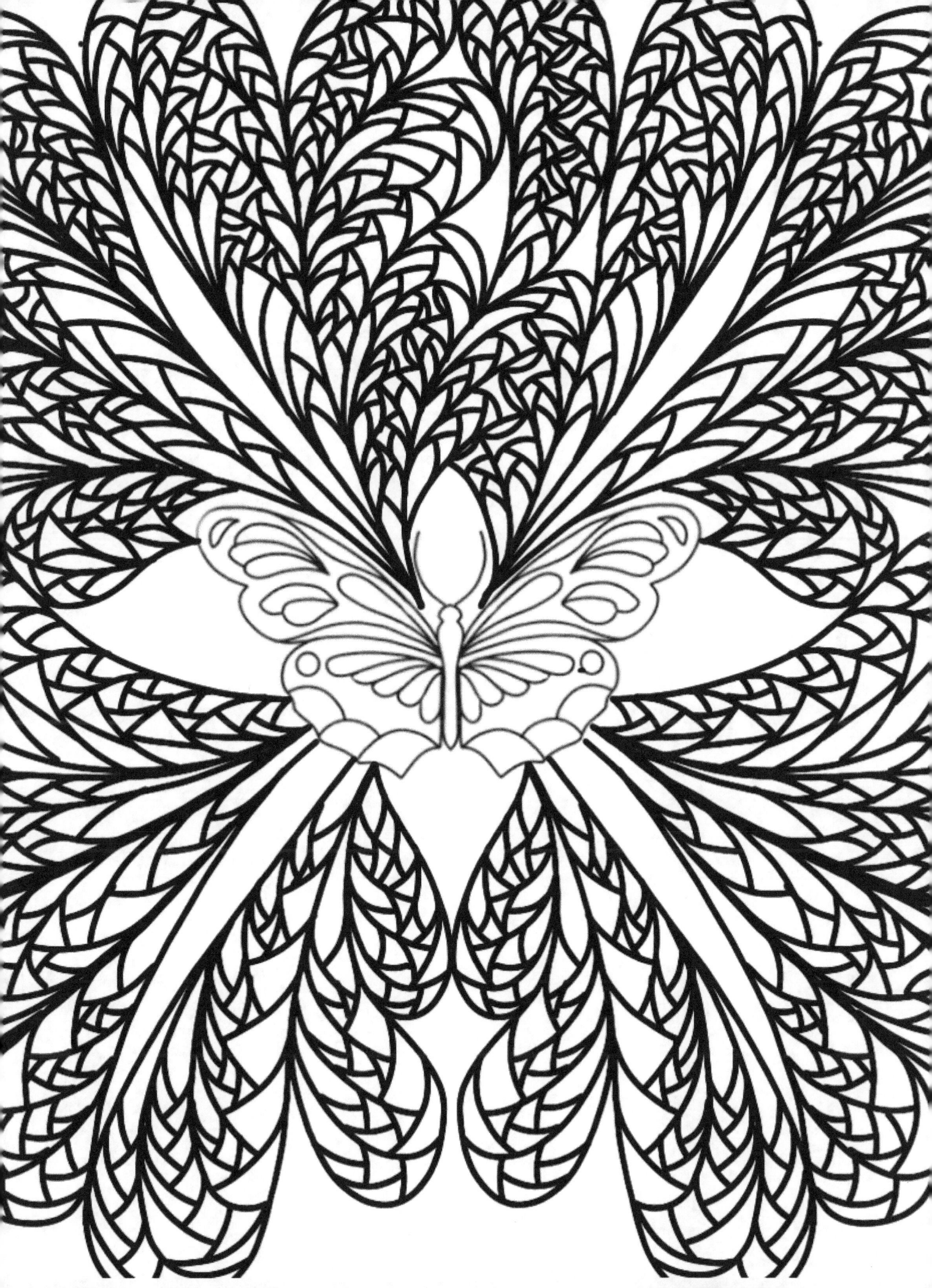

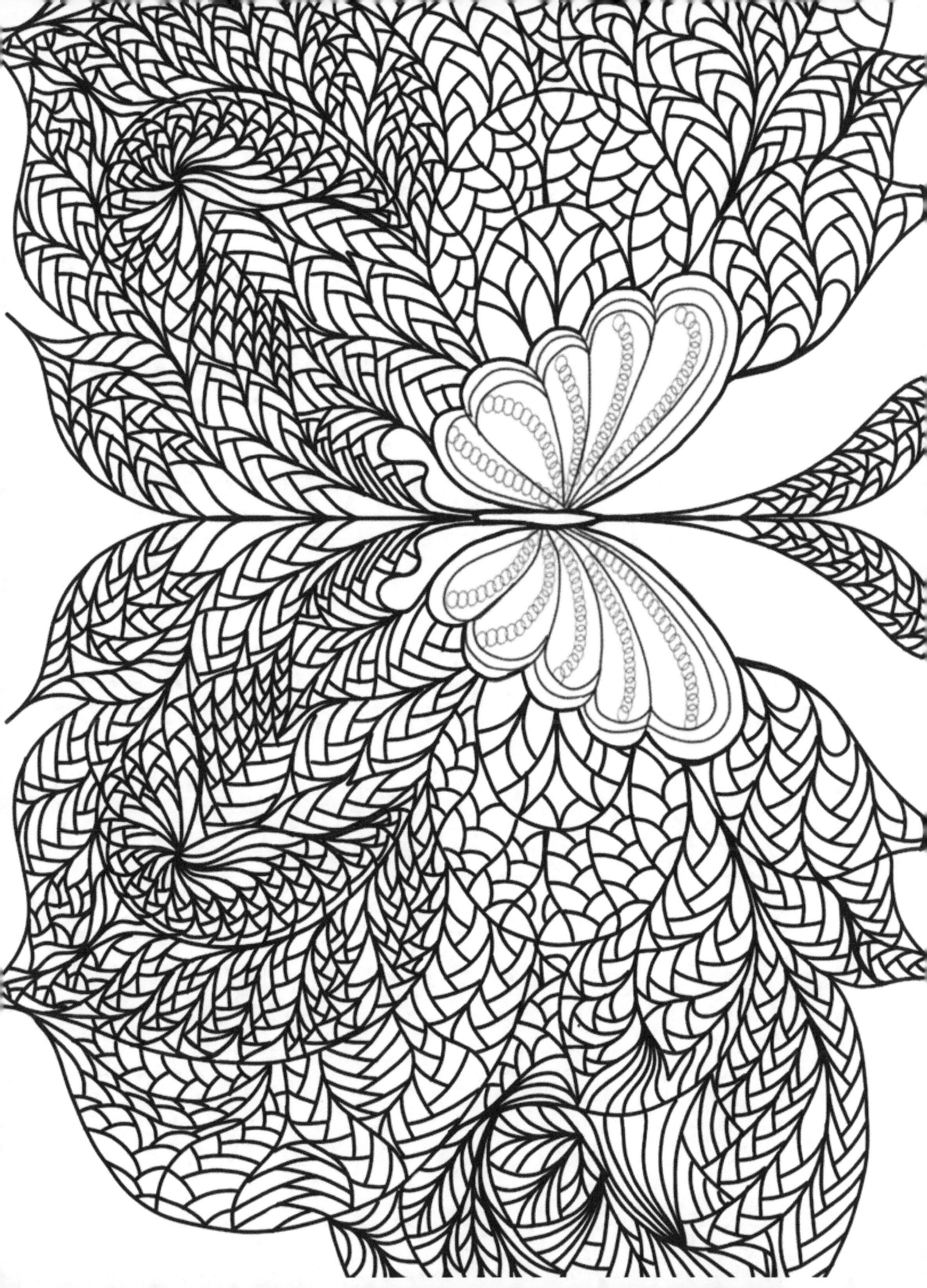

THESE BLANK PAGES ARE FOR YOU TO INSERT IN BETWEEN THE OTHER PAGES IN ORDER TO PREVENT BLEEDING OF MARKERS OR OTHER COLORING TOOLS ONTO YOUR OTHER DRAWINGS.

THESE BLANK PAGES ARE FOR YOU TO INSERT IN BETWEEN THE OTHER PAGES IN ORDER TO PREVENT BLEEDING OF MARKERS OR OTHER COLORING TOOLS ONTO YOUR OTHER DRAWINGS.

THESE BLANK PAGES ARE FOR YOU TO INSERT IN BETWEEN THE OTHER PAGES IN ORDER TO PREVENT BLEEDING OF MARKERS OR OTHER COLORING TOOLS ONTO YOUR OTHER DRAWINGS.

www.ingramcontent.com/pod-product-compliance
Lightning Source LLC
Chambersburg PA
CBHW080550190526
45169CB00007B/2713